FIT FOR THE MASTER'S USE

A Handbook for Raising Godly Children

by
Nancy Dufresne

Books by Dr. Ed Dufresne

Devil, Don't Touch My Stuff!
Faithfulness: The Road to Divine Promotion
Golden Nuggets for Longevity
How to be Rich God's Way
How to Flow with Anointings & Mantles
Praying God's Word
The Footsteps of a Prophet
There's a Healer in the House
Things That Pertain to the Spirit

Books by Nancy Dufresne

A Supernatural Prayer Life
Causes
Daily Healing Bread from God's Table
God: The Revealer of Secrets
His Presence Shall be My Dwelling Place
I Have a Supply
Responding to the Holy Spirit
The Healer Divine
There Came a Sound from Heaven:
    The Life Story of Dr. Ed Dufresne
Victory in the Name
Visitations from God

Dedication

I lovingly dedicate this book to my parents, Kenneth and Carolyn Chapman. I will always remember my childhood years and home as being full of happiness and love, and I'm eternally thankful to my parents for being that loving, sacrificing, guiding example of parenthood.

Kenneth and Carolyn Chapman

Table of Contents

Foreword

In writing this book, I certainly don't presume to be an expert on child behavior, but having been raised in a happy home with wonderful parents, having parented two sons, and having been a pastor in the family of God for almost two decades, I have learned a few things that can be of benefit to parents and a home. It's with this in mind that I share some of the truths and nuggets that will help parents to train children that are *Fit for the Master's Use.*

So whoever cleanses himself [from what is ignoble and unclean, who separates himself from contact with contaminating and corrupting influences] will [then himself] be a vessel set apart and useful for honorable and noble purposes, consecrated and PROFITABLE TO THE MASTER, FIT AND READY FOR ANY GOOD WORK.

(2 Timothy 2:21, Amplified)

Fit for the Master's Use

Chapter One

Serving God Together

Psalms 127:3, 5
*3 Lo, children are a heritage of the Lord and the fruit of the
womb is his reward.
5 Happy is the man that hath his quiver full of them… .*

God's design for the family is that they serve Him and fulfill His
plan together, and the home that puts God and His Word first will
produce children that will be a source of great blessing, and will
bring much pleasure and joy to the home and to others.

Those who are lost and without God in this world are not assured
of producing children that bring them joy. With no Biblical founda-
tion and Christian guidelines surrounding a child's upbringing, they
will be subject to any and all of this world's devices and traps, but
those who make Christ and obedience to God's Word the center of
their home, can count their children to be a daily joy.

Although life can accelerate to an overwhelming pace, we, as
parents, must always hold back on the throttle that would cause us to
pass up moments and times of training and enjoyment with our children.

Making time for our families is of prime importance, but make
no mistake about it – family time does not just mean playing games
together, having family outings, sitting together and watching television all evening, nor does it simply mean going to a movie theatre to
watch the latest movie. Family time may include some of these
things, but how wonderful to have your family time around church
and around the people of God, doing the work of God together. Train
your family to serve God together, working together in your local

church; this will be some of your richest family time and most valuable training for your children.

When I was growing up in the Methodist church, most of the work that needed to be done on the church building and the grounds was done by the church members. There was a man who came with his sons to work on the church lawn every Saturday. As a family, they served God and made ready the gathering place for God's people. This was not only a time to be with his sons, but it was a time to teach them the honor of serving God in any place there was a need. What a blessing that man and his sons were to the church family!

I began playing the organ in our Methodist church when I was in the 8th grade, and I played it until I moved away to college. I could always be found on that organ bench every time the church doors were open.

My mother taught us early that you didn't have to receive monetary payment from the church just because you served there in some way. The church offered to pay me for being the organist (when in reality, I probably should have paid them for listening to me), but my mother spoke right up, saying, "Oh, no, she won't be taking any pay from the church for playing the organ. The least she can do is use what she has to serve the church!" My mother taught us the value and the place of serving with no other motive than to be a blessing. Am I saying that it is wrong to receive money from the church for performing a service? Absolutely not, but it is wrong to teach our children to expect to be paid every time they lift their hand to serve God in some way. Teach them that it is a blessing to serve. Teach them to serve God together, side-by-side with you.

As a pastor, I firmly believe that serving in my local church when I was growing up was part of my preparation and training time for what I'm doing today.

To teach your children to serve God and bless others is one of the greatest things you can teach them, but it's only taught through you leading them by example. So, by all means, make your family time include a time of service to the Lord.

CUT THE CLUTTER FROM YOUR DAY

Our days are to be full as we live out God's plan; we are to be always abounding in the work of the Lord (I Corinthians 15:58). But we are not to live hectic lives, full of unnecessary things that lead us off course. Make the hectic life come to a stop so you and your family can serve God and fulfill His plan. You have to take charge of your day, or your day will take charge of you. You have to order your time, or your time will order you. Your day must carry an order and a discipline to it, but it must be an order that has God, the work of God, and His plan for your family as its focus. When you discipline yourself and order your day properly, cutting out the meaningless, time-wasting tasks, you will find the time you need for God and your family.

We must hold ourselves in check to not be too busy to train our children toward the things of God and toward God's plan for their lives. Yes, we find many responsibilities surrounding our daily lives, but we must take charge of our moments, and not live life at such a pace that our time with God, our spouse, children and loved ones are overlooked; these are to be enjoyed during the course of our day.

LOVE THE MOMENT

Don't be so busy that you lose out on the joy that belongs to today – the joy of your family and loved ones. Enjoy your children through all the many stages of their childhood. Enjoy the diaper stage, as well as the teenage stage, for they grow out of them all too soon. Enjoy the little hands that cling to the legs, and the scattered toys that lie around the house.

These are the days of your life. Live each moment to its fullest. It's right and good to be filled with hope and vision for what the future holds for us, but if we're not careful, we will fail to enjoy the glory of the moment we're living.

Enjoy your children. They are a blessing from the Lord. Train them according to God's Word and they will be a blessing to you all the days of your life.

Love is to find its richest expression and flow in your home, with those you love most – your own spouse and children – and live days of heaven on earth.

Chapter Two

Protect Your Home

This world is in great need of good examples to follow, for it's full of many who grasp hopelessly for life's meaning. Today's youth are flooded with images of the public figures who are flashed on the forefront of society as today's heroes, when in reality, the majority of them are lost, scattered, tragic figures. Many of their marriages, homes and private lives are in shambles, and today's youth receive mixed signals of what brings true happiness and joy to life.

It's into this confused, chaotic arena that the homes of Christian families are to rise up and sing openly as testimonies of how a God-filled home is to be a place of heaven on earth. We must always remember that the home of the believer is to be a shining testimony of God's grace, love, and power to a world full of hopelessness.

In the days of Noah, when the world was filled with all sorts of godless perversions and lifestyles, God saved a family. God found one God-fearing family amidst a degenerate world, and God was able to start all over again – just because He had one family who would not bow to the flow of the currents of the world surrounding them. May your family always qualify as being one that God is able to have as a shining example in this dark world of selfishness and sin.

In the days of Moses' birth, the Pharaoh sent out an order that all Hebrew baby boys were to be killed. When Hebrew boys were being slaughtered at the sword of the Egyptian soldiers, one family rose up and said, "Not in this house!"

Because they were not afraid to take a stand against the evil word sent out by the Pharaoh, God gave Moses' mother a plan that spared the life of her son.

When Moses went back to Egypt as an 80-year old man to lead

them out of slavery, he stood as the only man his age among all the Hebrew males, for all the others had been slaughtered at birth. All his days, Moses' life was an ongoing testimony to the generations of one family who would not yield to Pharaoh's destruction.

Even so, the home of every Christian should bear the same mark of being untouched by that which is destroying many homes in today's society. Every Christian family is to stand up in the face of all that is wrong, and proclaim, "Not here! You won't come into my home! We're doers of the Word!" Then that which destroys the homes of millions, won't gain entrance into your home. Protect your home from all that would divide it. God will hold that home in the safety of His power as those in the home will choose to live according to His Word.

The devil seeks to divide and destroy the home through strife, bitterness, unforgiveness or divorce, because then he can automatically weaken future generations. Every life void of a strong, secure homelife is like a tree with a twisted root system. A twisted home produces twisted children; their self-image is weakened, their minds are distracted, and their trust is shaken. Only the power of God can bring about the changes that will correct a life that has been robbed of a happy, secure home.

For those who have gone through divorce or come from divorced homes, God can restore and set on course the lives of those who are affected, but that is only as one becomes a doer of the Word in the face of every situation.

The home of the godly is a rare commodity in today's world, and the children that are produced from that home are a real treasure. The parents of a child either set the course of a child's life toward heaven or hell, and blessed is the child who finds his footsteps turned toward the narrow road that leads to God.

THE WAY THEY SHOULD GO

In speaking of Abraham, God said, *"For I know him* (Abraham)*, that HE WILL COMMAND HIS CHILDREN AND HIS HOUSE-HOLD AFTER HIM, and they shall keep the way of the Lord, to do justice and judgment; that the Lord may bring upon Abraham that which he hath spoken of him."* The Amplified Bible reads, *"...so that the Lord may bring Abraham what He has promised him"* (Genesis 18:19).

What a wonderful testimony God declared about Abraham! He knew Abraham would raise his children according to the Word of the Lord, and that he would also command that his entire household operate according to the Word of the Lord. God also stated that because Abraham raised his children right and conducted his household right, then He could bring His plan for Abraham's life to pass.

The Bible tells us to, *"Train up a child in the way he SHOULD go..."* (Proverbs 22:6). Not the way he wants to go, or the way his friends want him to go, but the way he *should* go. Yes, as parents, God will show you His plan for the life of your child and then He expects you to train your child in that direction. Teach your children that the only thing that will ever make them happy in life is to fulfill God's plan for their life.

Today's society will tell you, "Teach your kids that they can be anything they want to be!" That is not the training for the Christian home. There are a lot of people in this world who have become what they wanted to become, yet still live defeated, unfulfilled lives. It is not a man's plan for his life that builds happiness and success, but it is God's plan for a man that brings about a full, rich life.

Teach your children that th ey can be anything God wants them to be! What God has for them is far greater than anything they could desire or plan for themselves, and with God's plan is total fulfillment and blessing for everyone.

God's Word is the way they *should* go; God's plan for their lives is the way they *should* go. Training them in this is how you train your child in the way they should go.

Chapter Three

A Home of Honor

To have a household and to train children who are fit for the Master's use, we must not neglect the subject of honor. In today's society, honor has degenerated with each generation until it is something that is virtually non-existent in today's society.

Years ago, a man's handshake on a business deal was his contract. His word carried weight, and his word meant something. But living in a system that magnifies legal entanglements and slippery word games, a man's word has come to hold no value in society.

Even though this world's system sinks lower and lower in the value of a man's word, God's system still operates on the honor of words. The divine order of God is that He speaks, then He acts in line with what He spoke.

God's Word can never fail! His Word always comes to pass because of the honor of the One who spoke the Word. Psalm 138:2 tells us, *"...thou hast magnified thy word above all thy name."* Another translation of that verse reads, *"...for your promises are backed by all the honor of your name"* (The Living Bible: Paraphrased, Kenneth Taylor). The reason His Word is always good is because of how honorable He is. A man of honor can always be trusted and can be counted on to do what he says. This is even more so with God. He is perfect in honor. He has never failed one time to do as He said, and He has dealt honorably with every man.

Even though this world carries little honor with it, because we are God's children, He expects us to be honorable in our lives at all times, even as He is. The dishonor others may operate in will never release us from our responsibility to live lives of honor, for we belong to God, and God measures us according to His standard of honor, and not according to the lower standard of others.

All honor begins in the home. The level of honor in a home will never surpass the honor level of the parents. To raise godly children, you have to raise yourself. The level of honor one operates in must continue to grow all of one's life. The more one grows in God's Word and in his fellowship with God, the greater the level of honor he will live in.

If someone is honorable, they are honorable in every arena of life; they are not just honorable in selective situations, they are honorable toward all people in all situations.

What is our standard of honor? God's Word is our standard of honor. It does not matter how other people live and what their standards are; what matters is what God's Word says. That is what we are to live by. God's Word raises the standard of honor in your life. God's Word is the measuring stick our lives will be measured by.

HOW TO LIVE LONG ON THE EARTH

Ephesians 6:1-3 instructs us, *"Children, obey your parents in the Lord: for this is right. HONOUR thy father and mother; which is the first commandment with promise; THAT IT MAY BE WELL WITH THEE, AND THOU MAYEST LIVE LONG ON THE EARTH."*

To teach children to honor their parents is to keep them safe. To teach children to honor their parents is to teach them how to have things go well with them. To teach children to honor their parents is to teach them how to live long on the earth; it adds long life to them.

When our sons obeyed and honored us properly, then things went well for them. If they didn't obey and honor us as they should, things didn't go so well for them – they lost privileges and liberties they had previously enjoyed. When they obeyed and honored us, they received more blessings.

Honor keeps things in place so that all will go well with your child. Honor extends their life; it keeps them safe, and keeps the door closed to the enemy. Honor is crucial to living a long life.

A child is not born knowing how to honor; it must be taught to him. Don't expect honor to be taught to him by his peers, or by a society void of honor. It must be taught to him by his parents; therefore, honor must be a strong flow in the life of the parents – honor in every arena of life.

Parents are not perfect, so they will make mistakes. Children are not honoring a parent because they're perfect and always do everything right, but because their position of authority as a parent deserves honor and respect.

PARENTS WHO HONOR

As a parent, you want your children to honor you, but then you must look back and see if you are honorable toward our own parents; for what you sow, you will reap. The spiritual law of sowing and reaping does not only work for your finances, but it also works toward your relationships. Even if you were raised in a home without God and your own parents were not Christians, God still expects you to deal honorably toward your parents.

Being honorable toward your parents who may not be Christians does not mean to have fellowship with a godless lifestyle. It does not even mean allowing unsaved parents or family members to bring godless actions and activities into your home. It does not mean being permissive toward sinful practices they may participate in. But it does mean walking in love toward them, and acting honorably toward them, even if they are not always honorable in their actions toward you.

You may be giving yourself to going on with God, and they may be giving themselves to going against God, but you still are to be honorable toward them. If they do not serve God, it will affect how much fellowship you can have with them, but you still are to honor them. You can still let them know you love them, even if fellowship with them is difficult or rare. You can still speak well of them and toward them, refusing to magnify the negatives. You can communicate with them, letting them know your love for them, but avoid any topics of conversation that would lead to strife.

Living a godly life at all times is the best example they could ever have from you; that is the testimony that preaches the most to them. As you live a life of honor toward your own parents, then you can best teach your children what is expected of them toward you.

RIGHT SPEAKING IN THE HOME

A home of honor is a home where right words are spoken, and evil speaking against others is unacceptable. Honor will never speak evil of or criticize others, and would certainly never do it in front of children, for it can cause them to have a critical spirit. Honor is not permissive toward evil speaking, but it speaks well of others.

It's to be understood that as those in the home speak words of love, they keep the door closed to the enemy and, therefore, they also keep the door closed to sickness and disease. To step outside of love is to step into sin, and sin opens the door for the enemy to attack you.

To have a home of honor is to have a home of love, and that is how to keep a family healthy and happy.

HONORABLE TOWARD ALL

Those who are honorable in the home will be honorable in every arena of life – toward God's Word, toward the local church, toward one another, in the marriage, in conversations, in financial and business matters, in relationships – in every arena.

If a child is taught honor toward their parents, then that honor will automatically transfer toward God, their church leaders, their school teachers and all other authority in their lives.

HONORING THE BODY OF CHRIST & THE LOCAL CHURCH

There are two institutions on the earth authored by God: the family and the Body of Christ. These two must be priorities in our lives. Above all else, we must teach our children to always hold the highest honor for these two institutions – the family and the Body of Christ.

Train your family to always consider how their actions will affect the family, and how their actions will affect the Body of Christ. The decisions we make in life seldom just affect us, but they affect our loved ones, and they can have an effect on the Body of Christ. To sow hardship toward the family or toward the Body of Christ will cause one to reap hardship. To sow blessing toward the family or the Body of Christ will cause one to reap blessings.

Train your family to always hold the highest honor for the Body of Christ, God's family. You train them to honor the Body of Christ by training them to honor their own pastor and those in their local church.

The local church is like no other place on the earth. It is the place where you are to learn more about God, and learn how to live in a way that's pleasing to Him. It's the place where you are to learn His Word and learn how to fulfill His plan for your life. No other activity or function we're involved in is equal to what takes place in a local church where God and His Word are honored. *To attend church services is the highlight of the believer's week.* It's the place where God meets with His people unitedly. It's the place where revelation of His Word is to flow to meet the needs of the people. It's a place where sinners receive God's forgiveness, where backsliders come back to God, where broken bodies are made whole, where marriages and homes are restored, where children hear God's plan for their lives, and where answers for life are given. There's no place on earth like the local church where God and His Word are honored and magnified!

Pour this understanding into your children. Teach and train them of the great honor of belonging to the Body of Christ, and of being a co-laborer with God in the earth.

HONORING THE MOVE OF GOD

In Acts 10, we read of a man by the name of Cornelius. He was, *"A devout man, and one that feared God WITH ALL HIS HOUSE, which gave much alms to the people, and prayed to God always"* (Acts 10:2).

God had Cornelius to send for Peter, who would preach Jesus unto Cornelius and his house. While Peter was traveling to Cornelius' house, the Bible tells us, *"...Cornelius waited for them, and had called together HIS KINSMEN and near friends"* (Acts 10:24).

When Peter entered Cornelius' house, Cornelius told Peter, *"...now therefore ARE WE ALL HERE present before God, to hear all things that are commanded thee of God"* (Acts 10:33). Cornelius had brought his family and his friends together to hear what the man of God had to say; he was expectant that they were going to hear from God that day, and he wanted them all in on it.

Peter proclaimed Jesus to them, and Acts 10:44 tells us, *"While Peter yet spake these words, THE HOLY GHOST FELL ON ALL THEM which heard the word."* An outpouring of the Spirit of God came to Cornelius' house that day, and the Gospel spread to the Gentiles; it reached those who previously had no covenant with God.

Cornelius had raised his children in such a way that they received the move of God when it came to their home. Although they were not Jews, but Gentiles, Cornelius taught his family to honor and respect God. Because Cornelius honored God and had raised his children to honor God, his home became a place where God could pour out His Spirit. His future generations would carry on the outpouring of God that fell upon Cornelius' household that day. It didn't end with Cornelius; it moved into his children, then into future generations.

When you train your children to honor God and His movement, you place your household in a position to receive of heaven's outpourings.

What if Cornelius had not trained his children to honor God? Would his household have been visited as it was? It is very unlikely. The move of God comes to those who reach for it, to those who hunger for it, and to those who have honor and respect for it. Outpourings of God don't just flow randomly; they flow in an atmosphere prepared for them. We must train our children to hunger for and receive God's moving in our midst.

Parents either steer their children's steps toward heaven or hell. It takes active, diligent training to purposefully guide them in heaven's way, and it is every parent's responsibility.

You cannot teach your children to honor a God they can't see without teaching them to honor their parents, who they can see.

Do as Joshua did. He rose up and declared, "...as for me AND MY HOUSE, we WILL serve the Lord" (Joshua 24:15). Joshua let it be known that not only was he going to serve the Lord, but so were his children. He didn't leave it up to his children, asking them if they wanted to serve the Lord. He made the decision for himself and for his household. He trained them to serve the Lord.

HONOR & FAITH

Genesis 18:17-19
17 And the Lord said, Shall I hide from Abraham that thing which I do;
18 Seeing that Abraham shall surely become a great and mighty nation, and all the nations of the earth shall be blessed in him?
19 For I know him, that HE WILL COMMAND HIS CHILDREN AND HIS HOUSEHOLD AFTER HIM, AND THEY SHALL KEEP THE WAY OF THE LORD, to do justice and judgment; that the Lord may bring upon Abraham that which he hath spoken of him.

Abraham was a man of faith, and we see that by the way he trained his children and those of his household. Anytime you find a man of strong, robust faith, you find a man of honor. Faith and honor are inseparable. Without honor you can't have strong faith. Because Abraham would bring his children and household into this life of faith and into the way of the Lord, it put him in the position to receive all God planned for him; God's plan could be fulfilled there.

To raise children in an atmosphere of faith and honor is vital to their ability to move with God and to receive from God.

HONOR & RECEIVING

Mark 6:1-6

1 And he went out from thence, and came into his own country; and his disciples follow him.

2 And when the sabbath day was come, he began to teach in the synagogue: and many hearing him were astonished, saying, From whence hath this man these things? And what wisdom is this which is given unto him, that even such mighty works are wrought by his hands?

3 Is not this the carpenter, the son of Mary, the brother of James, and Joses, and of Judah, and Simon? and are not his sisters here with us? And they were offended at him.

4 But Jesus said unto them, A prophet is not without honour, but in his own country, and among his own kin, and in his own house.

5 And he could there do no mighty work, save that he laid his hands upon a few sick folk, and healed them.

6 And he marveled because of their unbelief. And he went round about the villages, teaching.

Because those of Jesus' hometown didn't honor Him, they were offended at Him; and because they were offended at him, they were in unbelief. The end result was that, *"...he could there do no mighty work... ."* It doesn't say He *wouldn't*, but He *couldn't* do a mighty work among them.

He couldn't do for them what He wanted to do for them. Why? Because they dishonored Him. God wasn't withholding His power from them; dishonor made them unable to receive it. Dishonor is like putting a lid on a vessel – nothing can get in. But honor opens one up to receive freely.

If those in Jesus' hometown of Nazareth would have honored Jesus, they would have received power that would have healed the sick and worked miracles. But many were deprived of receiving God's power because of dishonor.

To have a home of honor is to have a place where God's power and God's ability can flow freely and unhindered, for where people are honorable toward God and His Word, people are quick to believe and quick to receive from God.

Fit for the Master's Use

Chapter Four

God's Will for Your Children

John 4:34
*Jesus saith unto them, My meat is to do the will of Him that
sent me, and to finish His work.*

Jesus let us know that carrying out the will of God was the most
important thing in His life. What meat was to His body, the will of
God was to His spirit and life. Just as meat brought strength and nourishment to His body and sustained it, God's will was the nourishment
and the strength of His life. Jesus knew that the thing that sustained
His life was being in the will of God. That which kept Him in a place
of safety when being continually surrounded by opposition, was
being in the will of God.

Parents want the best for their children, and the best thing that you
could teach your child is that God's will for their life is the best thing
they could ever have. God's will is the place of protection and safety.
God's will is the only place of real fulfillment. Long life is connected
to God's plan. To veer away from God's plan is to veer away from
long life, but to follow God's plan is to stay with long life.

God's Word instructs parents to train up children in the way they
should go (Proverbs 22:6). God's will is the way they should go.
We're not to train up children in the way they *want* to go, but we're
to train them up in the way they *should* go. They *should* go the way
of the Word. We must train them that the way of the Word is the will
of God for their lives.

Before our oldest son was born, we knew what he was called to
do, so we trained him in that direction. When our youngest son was
ten days old, God told us what he was called to, so we're training him
in that direction. God will reveal to a parent what their children are

called to, for that knowledge helps parents to train them more fully for their call and purpose.

I've never told my children that they could be anything they wanted to be; rather I've told them that they can be anything God wants them to be. They never have to formulate a plan for their lives, for God has already authored a perfect one. What God has for our children is so much greater than anything else they could formulate for their own lives. What God has for our children will bring greater fulfillment and blessing to their lives and to the lives of others than anything else they could conjure up on their own. Many have gotten the things they wanted for their own lives, only to realize at the end of it all, that it fell short of fulfilling them.

God's perfect will for our lives will never leave us in an unfulfilled, empty place. Only in God's will is total joy, total fulfillment and total blessing. To accept anything less than God's perfect will is to accept less than God's best.

To start training our children when they are young about the grandness of God's plan for their lives is to give them a great advantage and a head start in life. As our children grow to know God's will for their life and fulfill it, it spares them much hardship and difficulties.

How can we know God's plan for our lives and the lives of our children? As we take time to fellowship with God through His Word and prayer, His plan will unfold to us; clarity will come to our spirits, then we can train our children in a way that will help them to hit the target and fulfill God's perfect will for their lives. (For more in-depth teaching on how to know God's will for your life, see my book titled *God: The Revealer of Secrets*.)

The parent is the greatest influence in the life of a child. To live your own life in line with God's Word and God's will is to set an example for them to follow, and it will influence your child toward God.

It is our privilege and responsibility to train our children so we can send them forth to fulfill God's plan for their life.

Chapter Five

Guarding the Fellowship of Your Children

As a parent and a pastor, I've seen that one of the most important things in the life of children and adults alike is their fellowship. Your life will go the direction of your fellowship. The lives of your children will go the direction of their fellowship.

When God wants to bless your life, He sends someone. When the enemy wants to harm your life, he sends someone. To guard your fellowship is to guard your life and the direction of your life. To guard the fellowship of your children is to guard their life and the direction of their life. Those you fellowship with are making deposits into your life, good or bad. *"Do not be so deceived and misled! Evil companionships* (communion, associations) *corrupt and deprave good manners and morals and character"* (I Corinthians 15:33, Amplified).

As we were growing up, my parents always let us know that our friends were welcome in our home, but we knew quite clearly what the guidelines were for choosing friends. On more than one occasion, mother let us know that our friends were welcome in our home as long as they were the right kind of friends. She also let us know in no uncertain terms that if she didn't think they were appropriate friends for us, she would send them on their way. To save ourselves from being embarrassed in this way, we made sure that our friends were someone she would approve of. We knew if she didn't approve of them, she would turn them out! Mother always made it clear to us from the time we were small what kind of friends she expected us to choose. (She didn't wait until we were teenagers to set down those guidelines for us. It just makes it easier for everyone to establish these things early in a child's life, rather than later.) If we did bring home someone she didn't approve of, she dealt with it immediately.

She didn't wait until we had been friends with someone for several months, and then make us end the friendship. She just knew it was better to not let it get started in the first place. Because of this, she kept a watchful eye on those we were hanging around with. She paid attention!

This is one of the most important jobs of parenting – paying attention. Parenting is all about paying attention. Pay attention to who your kids are talking to on the phone. Pay attention to whose house they're going to. Pay attention to who's visiting them. Pay attention! It pays in the end!

A RENEWED MIND

In raising our two sons, it was not enough for us that their friends be Christians, but they had to be young people who were having their minds renewed with the Word of God.

When anyone gets born again, their spirit is what got born again, but they still have the same mind they had before they were born again. Every Christian must take the Word of God and renew their minds. They must take the Word into their hearts and allow the Word to give them a new way of thinking, which will affect their behavior. When parents are renewing their minds with the Word of God, it will show up in their home and in the way they raise their children. Those children will have a head start, for they are being trained in line with God's Word.

Anyone who is a Christian, but fails to renew their mind with the Word of God, will still think and act the way they did before they were born again. It's important that a person be born again, but if they are to grow in their fellowship with God and experience success in life, they must renew their mind with the Word of God and be a doer of the Word, which will affect their behavior.

Any young person who wasn't being trained to live in line with God's Word was not appropriate fellowship for our sons. Our sons knew that it wasn't enough for them to have Christian friends, but their friends had to have proper fruit of Christian behavior in their lives.

Believe God for the right friends for your children, but don't allow them to hang around with the wrong kids just because you don't know of anyone suitable for them. Believe God for the right friends for them and He will send them.

When our oldest son was young, there was a time when we didn't know of many his age that were suitable for him as friends, but we didn't allow him to be with those who were unsuitable just so he could have friends. We prayed and believed God to bring him friends that would bless his life, and He did.

Your children will become what they fellowship with, so make sure that you approve of the behavior of their friends, for that's the behavior your own children will produce.

SUITABLE FOR YOUR CHILDREN

Our oldest son was especially active and into everything, although he could be rather quiet and not talk very much. So, we had to make sure that the friends he had were ones that didn't escalate his active behavior. If we put him with someone equally active, they would both go off the scale! One would egg on the other one, and then it was double the activity! It hyped him up too much, and created situations that were hard to handle; they would get into too much trouble together. We realized that the best companions for him were ones who were calm and easy going, for they would offset him and he would stay away from the edge of trouble. Our son always wanted to take the lead, so the best companions for him were ones who were willing to follow.

Our youngest son was more even in energy and behavior, so he played well with all kids – really active kids or with kids that were more laid-back in temperament.

You just have to pay attention to the type of temperaments in kids that bring out the best in your children, and who are the best suited to your own child. Again, it's not always best for your kids to have friends that are most like them, but rather have friends that bring out the best in them.

We always taught our sons that there's someone out there that we could all agree on to be their friends, and we all had to agree before a friendship could be developed.

FELLOWSHIP IN THE LOCAL CHURCH

We have taught our sons, as well as our congregation, that the highlight of the week is when we get to go to church. No job, no event, or no outing is as important as going to church, for our lives are centered around the Word and the local church. There's certainly nothing wrong with participating in other events and functions, but we keep those things in their proper place. The local church comes first, and then all other events come after that.

Our sons knew that if there was an event that conflicted with a church event, the church event came first. We never put sports practices and events before the local church. When our son was in sports, we let the coach know that he wouldn't be attending practices that happened on a church night. On a rare occasion, if something came up and they needed to miss a service, that was fine, for we weren't legalistic about it, but our spiritual habit was that church services and church events came first.

We understand that the local church is the place where the believer is going to receive help and answers for his life. God has given pastors to the Body of Christ to feed and guard them. It is the place where they can come and receive God's Word and answers for their life. It is the place where they can come on a consistent basis and have fellowship with those of like faith.

Because we understand and honor the role of the local church in the life of a believer, it is important to us that the friends of our sons have a good habit of church attendance. We know that if they are allowed to have close friendships with those who aren't faithful to a local church, those friends will pull them away from the church. Since the local church is so important to us and our family, that's where our sons find their best fellowship.

SURROUND THEM WITH FAITH AND LOVE

As I said earlier, it's always best to train children in line with the Word from the time they're born, but sometimes parents themselves don't get saved until later in life, and their kids are already teenagers or grown before the parents start walking in the light of the Word.

What does a parent do if their kids are older and haven't been trained in the way of the Word, and are rejecting the guidelines of the Word? Then that parent is to pray for them and say daily, "I surround my child with faith and love, and they'll turn out alright." Trust God to deal with them, and then refuse to worry about them. Cast the care of that child on the Lord, and then He will be able to work His holy influence upon them and make it easier for them to respond to God. But if you worry about them and you carry the care, then it will hinder God from moving in that situation. He moves in response to faith, not worry.

The Amplified Bible of Philippians 4:6 instructs us, *"Do not fret or have any anxiety about anything, but in every circumstance and in everything, by prayer and petition (definite requests), with thanksgiving, continue to make your wants known to God."*

First Peter 5:7 tells us, *"Casting the whole of your care [all your anxieties, all your worries, all your concerns once and for all] on Him, for He cares for you affectionately and cares about you watchfully"* (Amplified).

God doesn't want you to worry or carry the care about your children, but you're going to have to stay in faith for them by thinking faith thoughts and speaking faith words over them. Trust God to send the right people to your kids that can reach them with the Word. He knows who they'll listen to when they might not listen to you.

35

Chapter Six

Raising Children in a Local Church

There are two things that I've always emphasized as being of primary importance in raising children. The first thing is to closely guard their fellowship, for they will become like those they fellowship with. The second thing is to keep them plugged in and active in the local church.

By keeping them plugged in to a local church, you're keeping them in an atmosphere where God can reach them and minister to them. The atmosphere of a local church that preaches and teaches the Word, and honors the moving of the Holy Spirit is a setting that's conducive to ministering to those present, including your children.

In a place where the Word is taught and in an atmosphere of the anointing of God, your children can hear God's direction for their life. In that kind of atmosphere, they can see the power of God in manifestation in the services and it will feed their desire for the things of God; it will keep them from drifting toward the pull of the world. To raise children in a church where God's power is evident will leave its mark on them for the rest of their lives. That's why it's so important to keep them in the local church—to keep them in a place where the anointing and the power of God are in manifestation, and in an atmosphere where God can minister to them.

FINISHING THE RACE

Matthew 9:35 & 36
35 And Jesus went about all the cities and villages, teaching in their synagogues, and preaching the gospel of the kingdom, and healing every sickness and every disease among the people.

36 But when He saw the multitudes, He was moved with compassion on them, because THEY FAINTED, AND WERE SCATTERED ABROAD, AS SHEEP HAVING NO SHEPHERD.

The condition of these people who came to Jesus for healing was due to them not having a shepherd, a pastor. Not only were they sick, but this verse says they were fainting and scattered.

If a runner faints, he doesn't finish the race. There is a race that is set before all of us that we must run, but we're warned in this passage of scripture that those who don't have a pastor will faint during the course of their race; they won't finish their assigned course. They will faint and fall by the wayside before they cross the finish line. Yes, they will still go to heaven when they die, but they won't carry out and complete their assigned tasks on this earth.

The scripture also tells us that they will be scattered without a shepherd. Sickness can scatter their health, divorce can scatter their homes, lack can scatter their finances, and doubt can scatter their faith.

Too many times, we have only assigned these scriptures to adults, but not only do adults need a pastor, but our children and young people need a pastor. As a child grows up sitting under the anointing of a pastor, that pastoral anointing will flow into their lives and will keep them from fainting and keep them from being scattered; it helps them finish the race God has assigned for them to run.

PASTORING THE CHILDREN

During the course of pastoring, I was led of the Lord to make changes in our children's ministry. Instead of them being in their own classrooms for every service, on Sunday mornings I have those above the age of six to join us in our main service so that the children can be under that pastoral anointing, and then I have them to attend their own children's classes only during our midweek service. I want the children present in a service when the Word is taught under that pastoral anointing. I want them present in a service when the Spirit of God moves. I want the children to see people healed by the power of God. I want the children to see their own parents raise their hands and worship God. I want the children to be present when the Spirit of God moves across the congregation. I want the children to see people dance in the Spirit and fall out under the power of God. I want the children to run and dance in the Spirit. I want the children to learn to respond to the Spirit, as well as their parents.

I believe that if our children grow up seeing the genuine move of the Spirit, they won't be pulled off into the dangerous traps of the world, trying to find something to thrill them. They should grow up in a church that's full of the Word and full of the Holy Ghost, where God's power is in demonstration. When they have had a taste of God's blessing and power on their lives, they won't settle for the cheap, short-lived, superficial pleasures the world has to offer them.

Because the children are in our main service, I'm able to develop a rapport and relationship with the children, as well as with the adults. Then as those children grow into young adults, they will be more likely to stay planted in the church because they have a relationship with me as their pastor.

It's important that children grow up in a local church and have a relationship with their pastor, for their lives will experience the blessing and protection that flows from the pastoral anointing.

During our midweek service, all the kids go to their own classrooms for their teaching time. I value and appreciate all those who serve in teaching our children's classes that we hold during our midweek services, but as needed and as valuable as these precious teachers are to our church and our children, they can never take the place of the pastor and that pastoral anointing the children need to partake of.

Our Sunday morning service is the service I have chosen for all children above the age of six to attend. I don't mean to imply that all pastors should have this same format, but that's how the Spirit led us.

Some may think that children won't understand or receive anything in an adult service, but if the Word is taught as simply as it should be, everyone will be fed. When my mother would cook our meals, every age was able to eat something on the table. Even so, when the good Word of God is kept simple and fed under the anointing, all will be fed and be satisfied.

Since our kids join us in our Sunday morning service, we offer activity packets for our children to have during services and encourage them to draw pictures, or take notes on things pertaining to the services, then they can give them to me after the service or keep for themselves. When they bring their picture or notes up front to me after the service, they get a treat out of a basket of goodies we provide for them. This is something we have found to be fun and beneficial for them. We also encourage the parents to plan ahead for any items their children may need in the service so it will be fun for them.

When children attend services with their parents, the parents also have an opportunity to teach their children how to properly behave in this adult setting, as well as encourage them to participate in the flow of the services.

I also believe that our children bring a very special supply to the services. When Jesus was ministering to the crowd of over 5000 men (not including women and children) in the wilderness, Jesus wanted to feed them before they journeyed back home. A little boy with a lunch of loaves and fishes gave it to Jesus. Jesus blessed it and as the disciples distributed it, it multiplied, feeding the whole multitude, and there was much left over. That little boy brought a supply to Jesus and to the multitude that day that no adult brought. Children bring a precious, valuable supply to the church family.

Because children are hungry to learn, teach them to honor the Word and the local church, and teach them that they have a valuable supply to bring to their church family. They don't have to wait until adulthood to bring a supply to the Body of Christ; their supply is precious and valuable now.

If parents are faithful and consistent in their church life, and train their children to serve alongside them in their local church, it will affect the children. It will give them good habits toward the local church, and that good habit of church attendance will bless them all their life.

ATTENDING CHURCH ISN'T OPTIONAL

I grew up in a denominational church, and I always remember being in church. My mother never asked us if we wanted to go; we were going! My mother gave all four of us kids a good habit toward the local church. As a result, three of us are pastors, and my sister is active in her local church. That good habit mother gave us set our lives on a course that is helping us fulfill the plan of God for our lives.

The good habit of church attendance will have an effect on your child's future. It will be a place where they will mature spiritually, where they will see God's power in demonstration, where they will learn to walk with God, where their faith will be perfected, and where they will find fellowship with those of like faith.

Mother never asked us if we wanted to go to church. It was the law of our home – we were going to church! Even if we said we didn't want to go, that had no effect on her whatsoever! She was training us.

I've always been baffled by parents who ask their kids if they want to go to church. They don't ask them if they want to go to school. Yet, some parents treat church as though it's optional. School wasn't optional for us, and neither was church – we were going!

A child's spiritual welfare isn't optional; therefore, church isn't optional. That's the only place where children can be soundly educated in the Word of God. They need a pastor, and that can't happen without being faithful to a local church.

BE PREPARED

Another thing parents need to be mindful of is to properly prepare for church services. Since you know that your services are held every Sunday morning, then don't let the kids stay awake half of the night on Saturday night. Make sure they get enough rest, because it will affect how your family receives from God in the Sunday morning service.

In raising our sons, Saturday night was not the night there would be an all-night movie marathon. They could have kids over, but they couldn't stay up all night. The kids needed to be rested for church.

It's difficult to yield to God when you're tired, so in order to receive the most in a service, the family should be rested. Plan for that.

When we were growing up, on Saturday night mother prepared all of our clothes and laid them out for Sunday morning; then we knew there would be no last-minute clothing crisis.

When an event is important to you, you prepare for it. Church services are the highlight of our week and the most important events of the week, so we plan for it and we prepare for it. Then we can arrive to church on time without any crisis.

NEVER TOO YOUNG TO SERVE

When addressing the need of building into your children the good habit of faithful church attendance, we must also include the importance and necessity of teaching your children to serve in the local church.

Your children are never too young to serve and help in some capacity. Young children can help their parents who serve in the ministry of helps carry out their duties. An usher can take his small son with him to help straighten the items in the church foyer or sanctuary. A mom can take her small one to help pick up the toys in a classroom. Teach your children that they have responsibilities to help in the local church, just like they do in their own home. Young ones are expected to do small duties around their own home. Likewise, they should be taught the same thing toward the local church.

The majority of our congregation serves in our local church, and they have faithfully taught that to their children. We couldn't accomplish what God has given us to do without their precious, faithful supply.

There's one mom, in particular, who has taught her children the privilege and honor of serving in the local church. From the time they were old enough to walk, she kept them with her as she worked and served in the church, and she had them to assist her. They all would arrive early and stay late to do anything that needed doing in the church.

As a result of their faithfulness to God and to the local church, God blessed them with a new home on some acreage. They later built a pool in their backyard, and one day as they sat around the edge of the pool, she explained to her kids, "One reason God blesses us financially, so we can have these things, is because we serve in our local church." This mother has made the proper connection between their financial blessings and her family serving and being faithful to the local church.

Many Christians don't realize that their prosperity is connected to their local church. As they bless the local church, not only with their financial support, but also in serving in some capacity, they are measuring blessings and increase to their own lives. Many don't realize that the reason they have so many personal problems is because they don't make it a priority in their life to bring their supply to their local church, and they don't train their children properly towards the local church.

If parents don't train their children to be a supply to their local church, they are giving them bad habits that could stay with them their whole lives. But by training them in faithfulness toward God and the local church, they are setting them up for future blessings.

If you see a need to fortify this in your own family, you can start now. As you do, you'll see increased blessings.

God's Word tells us that those who honor God, He will honor. When we honor God by serving in His family, He will honor us. God's family is His priority; it must be our priority!

SIGN ME UP!

Our children have been active in the local church their whole lives. I didn't ask them if they wanted to; I just signed them up, and they were there.

You see, I grew up that same way. I remember being very young and going with my mother as she helped in the church or in the parsonage. She took us with her to help clean, paint or do whatever needed to be done.

I started taking piano lessons when I was 10 years old. When I was 13 years old, our church organist moved away, so the choir director asked my mother, "Do you think Nancy would play the organ for the church?

"She'd love to!" was her immediate response.

"Well, do you want to ask her?" he questioned.

"Oh no, I don't have to ask her. She'll do it!"

"We'd love to pay her," he added.

"No, you won't pay her," mom answered. "She can do that for her church without expecting to be paid." Mother was training me in the way I should go.

I did become the church organist, and I played for every service, wedding, funeral and choir rehearsal until I left for college. For a portion of my college years, I received scholarship money. I believe God blessed me with that because I served in our church faithfully without money being a motive.

It's not wrong to take a salary for work that you may do in a church, but if you'll be willing to serve faithfully, regardless of money, God will reward you. God rewarded me through a college scholarship that far surpassed any salary that church could have paid me.

When you love the Body of Christ and teach your children to love the Body of Christ, it will lead you to do something. You can't love without doing. Love will compel you to do.

We all have a supply God expects us to bring to the Body of Christ, for all Christians are part of this great Body. Many Christians don't realize it, but they suffer difficulties in different arenas of their life because of failing to bring their supply to the Body of Christ, but it's not too late to change that.

Be faithful to serve in the local church, and train your children in this great honor, and God's blessings will be apparent in your life, your home and family.

MAKE IT A SUCCESS

Growing up in our denominational church, I was active in the different departments of our church. When I was young, I was part of the children's department and participated in all the programs of that department. As I grew older, I then became part of the youth group. If the youth had a function, I was there.

There were times when some of the other youth didn't show up for a function, and when I would later see them and ask them why they weren't there, they would say, "Oh, I was on restriction and wasn't allowed to go." When mother would hear of that, it didn't set well with her. She would always say, "Those kids are part of that youth group and they have a responsibility to show up to the events. Don't those parents understand that the success of an event at the church depends upon the attendance of those kids? Those parents didn't just punish their child – they punished the whole youth group! Punish the child – not everyone else!" Mother made it clear to us that if we were put on restriction, she would do something that punished us, and not others.

As a pastor, I saw that same situation repeated. Parents would put their kids on restriction and keep them from coming to church events. The success of any church service or church event is dependent upon the faithfulness of its members. Punishing their kids by keeping them out of church functions is treating church as optional, and it's punishing the success of that event. Punish the child, not the event or others.

If your child is part of an event or a department, they ought to be there. That's how you train your children to keep their word. If you need to discipline your child by putting them on restriction, then restrict them in a way that doesn't affect others. Restrict them from the television, the telephone, the computer, or from outings with their friends, but don't restrict them from anything that they have responsibilities toward.

Train your child in faithfulness; it will affect their spiritual life, and it will help hold them steady in their adult life.

Faithfulness toward the Word of God and toward the local church is a key toward raising children that God can use in a mighty way.

Chapter Seven

Developing Your Child's Gifts

2 Timothy 2:20 & 21, Amplified
20 But in a great house there are not only vessels of gold and silver, but also [utensils] of wood and earthenware, and some for honorable and noble [use] and some for menial and ignoble [use].
21 So whoever cleanses himself [from what is ignoble and unclean, who SEPARATES HIMSELF FROM CONTACT WITH CONTAMINATING AND CORRUPTING INFLUENCES] will [then himself] be a vessel set apart and USEFUL for honorable and noble purposes, consecrated and PROFITABLE TO THE MASTER, FIT AND READY FOR ANY GOOD WORK.

Verse 20 tells of a home where there are gold and silver vessels, and also vessels of wood and clay. Verse 21 tells us what determines which kind of vessel you will be. Those who separate themselves from things that would corrupt become a vessel for honorable use. Those who don't separate themselves from things that corrupt will not be of the same use. It's not God who determines what kind of vessel we will be and what He can use us for – we are the ones who determine that. We are told to separate ourselves from corrupting influence. God isn't the One who separates us from wrong things – we are. God will lead us and deal with us to separate ourselves from things that would slow or hinder our spiritual progress, but *we* are the ones who must make the decision to separate ourselves. Those who obey God are the ones He can use.

Matthew 20:16 reads, *"...for many are called, but few chosen."* Why are only a few chosen since many are called? Because few will separate themselves to what God has called them to do. If people won't separate themselves, then He's not able to use them as He planned. To be called doesn't mean you're automatically qualified. You must qualify for what God calls you to. How do you do that? One way you do that is you separate yourself from that which would hinder or stop your spiritual progress.

Paul wrote to Timothy, *"Do not neglect the gift which is in you...Practice and cultivate and meditate upon these duties; throw yourself wholly into them [as your ministry], so that your progress may be evident to everybody"* (I Timothy 4:14 & 15, Amplified).

What was Paul telling Timothy to do? He was telling him to separate himself from things that would distract him from developing his gift so that he could become skillful and make progress in what he was called to do. When someone is giving themselves to developing their God-given gifts, then they will make progress, and that progress with be evident to others.

It's up to you to excel in what you're called to – it's not just up to God. He empowers you, but it's up to you to separate yourself from that which would hinder you so you can give yourself to something greater.

We know we must separate ourselves from things that are wrong, from things that would corrupt, but sometimes we must set aside or separate ourselves from legitimate things, things that aren't bad or wrong, but they just don't help us progress spiritually; they can be distractions from that which is more important. As Paul stated, *"All things are lawful unto me, but all things are not expedient* (profitable)... *"* (I Corinthians 6:12).

To be separated doesn't mean to be deprived. You're separating yourself from lesser things so that you can give yourself to greater things – things that will enhance your spiritual progress and your giftings; you're staying away from that which would hinder you.

When God tells us to separate ourselves, He's not seeking to deprive us or withhold anything from us, it's because He has more for us. He wants to direct us toward those things that will help us bear greater fruit in our lives. Separating yourself means to avoid that which isn't best so you can embrace that which is best.

Separate from lesser fellowship so you can have greater fellowship. Separate from lesser activities and interests so you can participate in greater activities and interests. Separate from things that hinder your abilities and gifts so you can participate in things that develop your abilities and gifts.

DEVELOPING GIFTS

Don't separate your child through depriving them or withholding from them, but give them something better in its place. It's not so much about separating them *from* something as it is about separating them *to* something. It's not about taking something *from* them, but about giving something *to* them.

That doesn't mean that children are to be deprived of doing natural things and having interests in natural things, but just don't neglect the development of the higher things – their giftings and abilities. Children should get to participate in different activities and events, but maintain proper balance and order, and make spiritual things the priority over natural things.

When I was young, my mother saw that I had some musical ability, so she put me in a position where that gift could be developed. She enrolled me in piano lessons, and then I became the church organist, which only increased my appetite toward music, which was a right appetite for my life. As a 10-year old, when I got home from school every day, mother made sure I practiced the piano for at least one hour.

What was she doing? She was separating me to what I was gifted for; then God could use me in that. There were things I had to give up to spend that time practicing, but it was necessary so that gift could be developed. She didn't wait for me to discipline myself to practice an hour a day. I didn't want to. I wanted to be outside playing, but she was steering me toward the development of that gift.

As parents, we need to recognize the gifts in our children and steer them toward the development of their gifts. As our children grow, they will seldom discipline themselves to develop their own gifts, so it will be up to the parents to put disciplines in place to ensure that their gifts are developed and nurtured. Mother watched over me to make sure I practiced daily. It required something of her to discipline me, but it paid off. It will require something of the parent to instill the discipline in your own child. If you don't, their gifts could go neglected and undeveloped.

OTHER INTERESTS

Mother allowed us to do other school and sports activities, but she didn't allow us to do them to the point that our real giftings were neglected. Some parents let their kids participate in activities and sports to such a degree that they spend their entire childhood and youth on those things, but as they reach adulthood, they have nothing to show for all that time they spent doing those extracurricular activities; those things never helped them develop the giftings and callings they were born for. Mother was very aware of this danger. She would let us participate in those activities to a degree, but she didn't allow us to spend so much time doing all those activities and then have nothing to show for it in the end.

It's important to know the giftings your child possesess so that you can steer them toward developing them.

EDUCATION

When it comes to your child's education, God will lead you to educate your children in a way that best suits them and what they're called to.

God dealt with us that our sons were to be either homeschooled or to have a private teacher throughout their school years. God led us to educate them privately, as opposed to putting them in a public or Christian school, because of what they are called to. There were times that our sons wanted to go to a regular school like other kids, but we had to stay with what God had led us to do. This was part of separating them to what they were called to.

We have always guarded their education and their fellowship, but they were never deprived in those areas, for we made sure they had proper schooling and proper fellowship that would enhance their lives and what they are called to do.

As a parent, God will direct you on the best route of education for your child, whether that be in a public or private school setting. As you follow His direction, it will prove to be the most suitable and best for your child.

WRONG APPETITES

When raising your children, it will be your responsibility to keep the wrong things away from so they don't get pulled off course by someone or something that would take them a wrong direction. You will have to make decisions for your children that may not be very popular with them, governing what they can or cannot participate in, until they learn to make the right decisions for themselves.

Some parents will say, "Well, my kids need to learn to make decisions for themselves." Well, they can only do that after they've been properly taught how to make right decisions. If a young person is repeatedly making wrong decisions, then they're not trained yet, and decisions may need to be made for them until they know how to make right decisions.

Kids and young people have to be protected from going wrong directions. Oh, yes, they may not like it when you put a halt to them doing something they want to do, but you have to be willing to let them be upset with you rather than let them go the wrong direction. They'll get over being upset, but they might not get over going the wrong direction.

Years ago, a mother asked me if I thought she should let her daughter participate in a particular event.

My question to the mother was, "Is that what you want your daughter to do? Do you want her to become part of that industry? Is that the direction her life should take?"

"No," she replied, "I don't."

"If you let her do that event, then she may get an appetite for it, and then you might not be able to get her out of it." The mother saw the point I was making. I was helping her to keep her daughter separated from the things that would pull her the wrong direction. You can be around the wrong things and get an appetite for the wrong things, and then you'll be pulled off your course.

Realize that what you allow in the life of your children, they will develop an appetite for, good or bad. The activities you let them participate in will give them an appetite for more. The kids you let them fellowship with will give them an appetite for more. So, make sure that you are giving them an appetite for the right fellowship and the right activities. Once an appetite is developed for wrong things or unprofitable things, it can be difficult to separate them from that.

Make sure you are surrounding them with the things that will help them fulfill what they're called to, and help them develop an appetite for the things that will aid them in fulfilling God's plan for their lives.

Chapter Eight

Parenting – It's Not a Popularity Contest

You can't be a good parent by trying to win a popularity contest with your kids. You're going to have to establish guidelines and boundaries that, at times, may not make you popular with them. There may be times they're unhappy with you because of the guidelines and boundaries you establish for them, but you have to be willing to let them be unhappy, rather than compromise what you know is right for them. Don't let their attitude sway you from what you know is right for them.

There were many times that our sons weren't happy with our guidelines, but we were willing to let them be upset with us rather than let them go the wrong direction.

A PARENT FIRST, NOT A BEST FRIEND

I am first and foremost a parent to my children – not their best friend. It's not my job to be their best friend; it's my job to train them in the way they should go.

It makes for an unhealthy relationship for a mother to try to fit in as "one of the girls" in the circle of her daughter's friends. A mother who tries to do that will find herself failing to act as a parent, and becoming wrongly permissive toward her daughter just to maintain a friendship status with her.

Parenting is no popularity contest. It is a full-time job that requires a parent to pay attention. As with anything, the better you pay attention, the greater your success rate.

Fit for the Master's Use

Chapter Nine

Family & Finances

So many lives and families are taken off course due to financial pressures. Sometimes, it's thought that God is only interested in the things that pertain to your spiritual life. Your spiritual life is of utmost importance because it affects every other arena of your life. But God is not only interested in your spiritual life – He is interested in every arena of your life. If it pertains to you, God is interested in it.

As a parent, I am interested in the spiritual lives of my children, but I'm also interested in everything that pertains to their life. It matters to me that they have the things they need and desire. It matters to me that they have money for their mortgage, clothing, food, and all their needs.

God is no different; God wants you blessed. He wants you and your family to have the things that you need and desire. God wants you blessed financially; He wants you to have every need supplied.

God also wants you blessed because those who are blessed financially are able to *be* a blessing financially.

God gives us all things richly to enjoy – not so these things can be served, but so they can be enjoyed (I Timothy 6:17). If we're not careful, we can begin serving the things that were only meant for our enjoyment, and end up neglecting those we love, and neglecting the people we are to bless.

Proverbs 10:22 tells us, *"The blessing of the Lord, it maketh rich, and he addeth no sorrow with it."* When God increases you, He won't steal from one arena of your life to increase another arena. When He blesses you financially, He won't have to steal from your spiritual life, from your church life or from your family life to bless you financially. He adds no sorrow with increase. When God blesses you, every arena of life increases.

To get a promotion and pay raise that causes you to have to miss church and neglect your family is not God's prosperity, for God's prosperity prospers every arena.

It's reported that financial problems are the number one reason for most divorces. How tragic this is, for money is so temporal; it can be easily gained or lost. It's heartbreaking to lose a home and a family over something so temporal.

Make money your servant in this world, for you must have it to function in this realm, but never let it be your master – it makes such a cruel one. Money is a tool, nothing more. Too many serve money, and spend the whole of their time and energy in accumulating it, but in the process, they lose their marriage, children and all in life that's really valuable or that holds any worth.

God has pleasure in the prosperity of His servants (Psalms 35:27), but Bible prosperity includes the prosperity of your spiritual life, your family life, and every arena of your life – not just financial prosperity. Yes, in our finances we are to show ourselves faithful to God, but never has God's plan included neglecting Him, spiritual things or family for the sake of accumulating money.

"But seek ye FIRST the kingdom of God, and His righteousness; and all these things shall be ADDED unto you" (Matthew 6:33). To seek first the kingdom of God is to put spiritual things first, for God's kingdom is a spiritual kingdom.

The divine order of increase is seek God's kingdom first, then the increase of things will follow. But when you place the increase of things first and neglect spiritual things, your life will get out of order and you'll open the door to the enemy; then there will be a subtraction from you. If you put money first, you're in danger of losing much – including your family. As you put spiritual things first and make God's kingdom your priority, God will add the things you need to you.

Put spiritual things first – your fellowship with God, feeding on

His Word, serving His family in the local church, and fulfilling God's plan for your life and family – and the things needed and desired in life will be added to you.

Without realizing it, marriages, families and children are being sacrificed for financial reasons. Realize that having a second car in the driveway, having a bigger home and more furniture isn't near as important as having children that are happy, peaceful, secure, and taught in the things of God. Those things don't mean prosperity without the prosperous family.

Eliminate the unnecessary things from your life that steal your time away from you and your family. Investments in your family and your children are some of the best investments you can make, and they yield far greater dividends than other things you could ever invest in.

Fit for the Master's Use

Chapter Ten

Supernatural Help

One of the greatest benefits of being born again and filled with the Holy Spirit is that you have divine help in your life, including in parenting.

The Holy Spirit has been my precious Helper so many times when I needed help and counseling as a parent. As I looked to the Greater One who is in my spirit, He always provided the help and the clarity I needed. At all stages and seasons of parenting, the Holy Spirit's guidance has made all the difference, so I can't overemphasize the importance of being sensitive to the Holy Spirit when faced with different situations as a parent.

When you follow the guidance of the Holy Spirit, you can know what to do in every circumstance of life. You won't have to resort to a "trial & error" method. The Holy Spirit knows what will get the best results when dealing with your children, and He will guide you. The Holy Spirit knows what method will reach your child and what will draw the proper response from them.

When looking to the Holy Spirit for guidance, take time to pray in the Spirit, speaking in other tongues. As you do, the Holy Spirit will communicate your answer to your own spirit, and then your answer will float up from your spirit and enlighten your mind. If your mind is too occupied or distracted, you could miss what your spirit is endeavoring to get across to you. In order to hear what your spirit is communicating to your mind, you must quiet your mind as you pray in other tongues. The best way to do that is to focus on your spirit as you pray.

In every situation of life, you can know the guidance of the Holy Spirit if you will daily take time to feed on the Word and pray in the Spirit.

In dealing with our sons, there were times I would have handled a situation one way, but the Spirit checked me, and I was led to handle it differently. When I followed the Spirit's leading, the right results were always reached.

The Holy Spirit is your Helper; look to the greater One within.

Chapter Eleven

Love & Authority

Love is protective, not permissive. Love carries great strength with it, not weakness. As a parent, you will need the strength love gives so that you can stand your ground and not yield to a more convenient route.

Love won't yield to a route for your child that isn't best for them. When you love a child, you do what's best for that child, not what's most convenient for you as the parent. In the end, it's always more convenient to put forth the effort to raise a child right, than to neglect proper training and end up with the difficulties that come from a child left untrained.

God is love, and He has a perfect society in heaven, yet even in His perfect society, one time, things tried to get out of order when Lucifer rebelled against God. God, who is love, rose up – love rose up and kicked him out of heaven. Love isn't permissive toward wrong doing. Love protects by exercising its authority properly.

When things try to get out of order in your home or family, love must rise up and say, "Not here!" Love will put things in proper order and hold them there; love won't permit disorder.

Some parents pray, "God, do something with my child." He did! He gave them a parent! God has authorized you to exercise authority over your child for their proper training. Take your place in your authority, and don't share the authority with your children – it's all yours!

In desperation, other parents may pray, "God, I give You my child to do something with," thinking that dismisses them from having to deal with the issues that arise. You can't give your child to God to raise. He gave them to you to raise. He won't raise them, but He will give you the wisdom and the understanding of how to raise them if you will be a doer of the Word and look to the help of His Spirit.

God has bestowed upon every parent the authority to protect their children from that which is wrong; that is love in action. To properly discipline a child is to love them. Love is not permissive toward wrong doing. That proper exercise of discipline will protect your children and keep them safe.

LOVE IS BALANCED

Love carries a proper balance. It not only exercises authority as it's needed, but expressions of love and affection should flow freely and be seen in the daily moments of life with your family through your words and actions. Love shows great joy just to be in their presence and fellowship. Don't limit the enjoyment of being with your family to special occasions, but learn to enjoy the moments of being with your family every day. Some of the fullest pleasures, the richest rewards, and the greatest privileges of your life are the moments you get to be with your family.

Chapter Twelve

Discipline & Tales From Home

Any parent who has more than one child knows how different each one of them can be. Their temperaments, personalities, and ways of thinking can be so different from one another. Because of that, the way to discipline each child can also be so different, because what works with one child won't always work with another. It will be the parent's adventure to find what best produces the right behaviors and responses with each child.

My mother always used to tell us, "Kids are smart, but you have to be smarter!"

When our first son, Stephen, was young, I was grateful for the many times I could pick up the phone and call my mother. "Mother, Stephen's doing this or that. I've tried everything I know to get him to stop, but nothing has made a difference. Nothing's working!"

"Nancy," she would reassure me, "if one thing doesn't work, try something else. Something will work!" Then she would proceed to give me ideas that I had never thought of. She just had a lot of common sense when it came to handling children.

"ONE, TWO, THREE…"

Mother had taught us long ago that if it was necessary, you should spank your child, but she also taught us that there are many other things you can do to get results.

When we were growing up, mother taught us as children that when she said something, she expected us to do it. If we didn't do something when we were told, she would hold up her fingers and begin to count, "One, two… ." When she reached "two" she was on her feet and on her way to you! If she ever had to reach "two", you had gone too far! With her, it was just best to move when she told you to do something, but if you felt really brave and wanted to push it, then you're bravery left you when she counted, "One!"

Because mother was so consistent (which is a key to good parenting), she didn't often have to spank us. We learned young that she meant what she said, and it saved us from having a lot of trouble and from having to be spanked very often. Mother was so consistent that we knew we couldn't get by with much, so we quit trying.

The more consistent you are as a parent to enforce the guidelines, the easier you make it on yourself and on your kids, for then they will stop trying to cross the boundaries as much when they know you'll be there waiting for them on that boundary line.

There are times you will have to spank your children, and it's for their own good. But as a parent, I soon came to see that if you're constantly spanking your kids, something is wrong. Some think that spanking is the only measure of discipline to use, but there are other disciplines you can use that may work better for some children. So, try different approaches if one approach isn't working.

Now, I do realize that because the temperaments of some kids are more high strung, they end up pushing the boundaries more, and they seem to require more discipline than other kids. Our oldest son required more discipline, and when he was younger, it seemed that a spanking was in order most days. But you do have to be aware that you can spank a child so much that it won't mean a thing to them, and then it does more harm than good, not getting you the desired result. You will have to find the means of discipline that gets you the desired result.

SOMETHING WILL WORK!

When Stephen, our oldest son, was about five years old, I would tell him to do something, and if he didn't like it, he would jump up and down in protest. He was always high energy and busy, but even this little fit was new for him as a five-year old. So, the first few times he did it, I would spank him, but he would do it again. That's when I called mother.

"Mother, I'm spanking Stephen when he throws a fit and jumps up and down, but he just does it the next day. Spanking isn't working."

"Nancy," she would instruct, "something will work. You've just got to find what will work. When he's jumping up and down, he's in control. *You've got to take the control away from him.* Have him to stand in a corner and jump up and down for 5 minutes as hard and as fast as he can. Then if he stops before the 5 minutes is up, spank him. When you make him jump up and down, then he's not in control anymore and he won't like it, so he'll quit doing it."

Well, that's what I did. The next time he jumped up and down throwing a fit, I said, "Okay, you want to jump up and down; then you're going to jump up and down as hard and as fast as you can for the next 5 minutes, and don't you stop. If you stop, then you'll get spanked." So, for the next 5 minutes he jumped up and down – not because he wanted to, but because I told him to. He realized that it wasn't as fun then, so he quit throwing that fit – he never did it again.

Mother was right. Something worked – we just had to find out what that something was.

That was a big lesson for me. When he wasn't in control, he wasn't interested in doing it anymore. *I learned the best way to get results was to take the control away from him. I had to stay in control.*

Didn't Have to Wait For Daddy to Get Home

When we were growing up and needed to be disciplined, mother never told us, "Just wait until your Daddy gets home!" She was home! And she knew how to handle us when we got out of line.

Daddy worked for years at an automotive supply store, and then he would go straight from his day job to working on his farms until early in the morning; then he would get up early the next morning and do it all again. He did that for almost 20 years.

Daddy worked such long, hard hours that he wasn't home much. If we ever complained about daddy being gone so much, mother wouldn't put up with it; she would straighten us out. She would always remind us how hard daddy worked so we could have a home, food, and the clothes we needed; she knew how hard he worked for his family.

It's detrimental to a marriage and to children to have a spouse complain about the other spouse, especially in front of children. Any issues that may arise in a marriage must be resolved privately, and must never involve the children; never allow them to overhear any disagreements. To involve children in disagreements in the marriage will cause greater damage in children than many realize.

Because daddy had to be gone from home so much of the time, mother was the one who did the majority of the disciplining of the children – and she was more than capable to do it. She knew how to handle us.

APPROPRIATE DISCIPLINE

There were times that we crossed the line and mother had to spank us, but she did it in an appropriate way. She spanked us on our bottoms; she didn't hit us on our backs or heads or in an inappropriate way, and she didn't use inappropriate items to spank with. She always spanked us in a way that was respectful toward us and not in a way that was degrading to us. She didn't try to embarrass us by spanking us in front of our friends; she was fair to us. She would certainly correct us in front of our friends if we needed it, but she never did anything to embarrass or to demean us.

Have you ever noticed that to raise kids properly, you have to raise yourself properly? You have to bring your own temper in line, and you have to deal with them in a way that makes a positive difference.

HOW TO RESPOND TO DISCIPLINE

If I needed to spank my boys, I never once had to chase them around the house. They didn't take off running or hiding from me when they knew they were getting a spanking. I had trained them how to respond correctly to discipline. I would tell them, "You go to my bedroom and lay across my bed, and I'll be there in a minute." A few minutes later, I would walk into my bedroom and they would be there waiting for me. There was no drama show going on. There was no yelling and screaming, no falling to the floor in drama, or chasing them around the house like a rabbit.

Before I ever spanked them, I would tell them why they were getting spanked, how many spankings they would get, and what I expected of them after they got spanked. I wasn't going to allow them put on a show of crying, falling to the floor and thrashing around. Children have to not only be disciplined properly, but they have to be taught how to respond properly to discipline. If they responded properly to discipline, it made it easier for them.

I do realize that some children are more high strung and dramatic than others and it can be a challenge to temper them because they don't always respond very calmly. But parents still must teach a child how they ought to respond to discipline, although it may take much reinforcement.

BE FAIR

My mother always emphasized being fair with us. Before we went somewhere, she told us ahead of time what she expected of us, which cut down on a lot of conflicts and difficulties.

If you'll let your children know ahead of time what you expect of them, and be consistent with your expectations, then you're being fair toward them, and it will help them comply. But to be vague and unclear about what you expect, then punishing them because they don't comply isn't fair. It's unfair to punish or spank a child for something if you didn't make it clear to them ahead of time what you expect of them.

I remember times when mother would take us to the grocery store with her, and even before we got out of the car, she would turn and talk to us; she would tell us what she expected of us when we got in the store. "You stay with me. Don't wander off. It's your job to stay with me; it's not my job to hunt you down. Don't go down the toy aisle; you're not getting a toy today. Don't put things in the grocery cart that you want. I am the one who puts items in the cart, not you. If you don't mind me, when we get back to the car, you will be in trouble. Now, do you understand me?" We understood!

By telling us what she expected of us ahead of time, then we didn't create embarrassing scenes in the store; we knew better. To let children know what you expect of them ahead of time is being fair to them.

My Piece of the Pie

There are many favorite stories of mine that mother tells about raising the four of us, and one of them is about my two older brothers.

When they were about eight and nine years old, they were fighting over the last piece of pie. Mother came into the kitchen and heard them arguing. She knew how to resolve it.

"David, you cut the pie into two pieces, then Dick, you pick which piece you want." David protested, "I'm not cutting it!" He must not have trusted his ability to cut the two pieces evenly since he didn't get to choose first.

"Alright," mother said, "Dick, you cut the pie into two pieces, and then David, you pick which piece you want."

But Dick protested, "I'm not going to cut it!" He must not have trusted his cutting ability either.

"David, you're not going to cut it?" mother questioned.

"No, I'm not!"

"Dick, you're not going to cut it?" she asked.

"No, I'm not!"

"Alright then!" So, mother picked up that last piece of pie, shoved it in her own mouth and walked off! Problem solved!

My brothers stood there stunned!

NO STEWING HERE!

If we got in trouble, mother wasn't one to send us to our room, she said, "Why would I send you to your room to stew and let you sit in there alone thinking how mad you are at me for you getting in trouble?"

No, if we got in trouble, she made us stay right in the same room with her until we got over it. She knew we would get over it quicker if we weren't left alone to stew over it.

PAYING ATTENTION

Mother believed in keeping us together as a family. She didn't often allow us to go sit in our bedrooms alone with the door shut. She kept us together in the family room, doing things together as a family, and then she knew what we were doing.

If we did go into our rooms, we had to leave the door open, unless we were dressing or sleeping. She saw it as her foremost job to pay attention to what we were doing, who we were with, or who we were talking to. She paid attention.

We were allowed to have friends over often, and we sometimes stayed all night with our friends, but only with those whom she knew. She had to know the kids and their parents well before we were allowed to spend the night with them, and then she had to know who all would be at the place where we were spending the night. She paid attention.

MAJOR ON THE MAJORS & MINOR ON THE MINORS

One thing mother emphasized to me when my sons were young was, "Major on the majors and minor on the minors." She knew that it was easy to make a big deal over something that wasn't really a big deal. When you're in the middle of an incident with your children, it can look bigger than it really is, and so you have to make sure that things are kept in their proper perspective. Don't make it a bigger deal than it is. Life will offer you enough issues without creating them, so don't blow them out of proportion.

WHERE ARE THE BOUNDARIES?

Mother always told us, "A smart kid is going to find their boundaries." She knew that as kids get older they are going to push the line of their boundaries to see how far they can go. She taught us that didn't mean they were a bad, rebellious kid, but it was part of the maturing process.

Yes, you will have to back them off the line when they start pushing the boundaries, which will require diligence on your part, but most every kid is going to push the boundaries in some way; that doesn't mean they're bad. Just make sure that when they get to those boundaries, they run into their parent who backs them off the line into the safe zone.

MAKE IT CLEAR

Before disciplining our sons, I would always make sure they were clear about why they were being disciplined. I brought them to the place where they acknowledged their own wrong doing, and that the reason they were being disciplined wasn't because I was upset, but because of something they had done.

Ephesians 6:1-3 reads, *"Children, obey your parents in the Lord: for this is right. Honor thy father and mother; which is the first com-*

mandment with promise; THAT IT MAY BE WELL WITH THEE, AND THOU MAYEST LIVE LONG ON THE EARTH.''

I would remind them that I want things to go well for them. I don't want them to face difficulties and problems unnecessarily, and that if they will respond properly to what they're told to do, they will avoid difficulties and they'll live long, happy lives.

Fit for the Master's Use

Chapter Thirteen

The Teenage Years

As kids enter their teen years, they start to see themselves in a whole new light. They become aware of themselves in a way that they weren't before, and this can be very interesting for them and for those around them. They are exiting childhood, and adulthood is within view, so this transition can prove to be eventful in many different ways.

As your young person embarks on this journey through these transitional years, it can seem as though you don't recognize the person they are becoming, for there is little similarity to the young one you were so used to. This is all part of the process and part of this season of their life. Just remember that you were once their age, and that these years aren't always the easiest to navigate through – everything is so new to everyone, to the child and to the parent. There's much growing going on, and much learning to do for everyone.

The young person is looking to express themselves as a young adult, and the parent is having to learn to no longer see them as the young child they once were. The young person is stretching to reach forward into who they will become, and the parent is reaching to try to keep up with who they are becoming.

Just as a child passes through many different seasons as they grow, a parent passes through many different seasons just to parent them, and it's new territory for everyone. The situations and challenges you face will be new for everyone, but the rewards can be rich.

WATCHFULNESS

As kids get older and enter their teen years, parents have to stay alert and pay attention as never before, for during the teenage years, some decisions and choices are made by them that can affect the rest of their lives.

These aren't to be worrisome years, but they are years that will require your watchfulness. These are not years to be feared or dreaded, but your diligence and watchfulness must continue. As you see your teenagers grow and mature during these years, it can be greatly rewarding.

As kids grow, they want more freedoms and liberties, and their circle of friends may widen. That's why it's more crucial than ever to keep them active in their local church, and with other Christian kids in the church whose minds are being renewed with the Word of God.

Establish the guideline that as the parent, you must be in agreement with any selection of friends. The earlier this is established in the life of your children, the easier it will be to enforce as they grow.

Their fellowship during these years is so important, for it only takes one wrong companion to take them off course. But being watchful over them and following the guidance of the Holy Spirit will serve to keep them on track.

The best way to be watchful as a parent over your teenagers is to do things together as a family; do things together that interest them. Yes, they need to have friends, but they don't stop needing their family. It's easy to watch over them when you're spending time with them.

THE HELP OF THE HOLY SPIRIT

In relying upon the help and guidance of the Holy Spirit, He may "check" you on a friend your child may bring home. You may not know why, but you just have a "check" in your spirit about letting your child develop a friendship with a certain person. If that happens,

74

follow that "check". When you get a "check" in your spirit, it's like getting a red light; you may sense an uneasiness or a hesitancy in your spirit about the situation. Follow that. It will serve to protect you and your child.

If you get a "check" in your spirit, the natural tendency may be to try to figure out why you got that "check". Many times, you may not know why, but don't dismiss it; you don't have to know why you have that "check" before you obey it.

If you get a "check" in your spirit about someone, it doesn't necessarily mean that they're a bad person, but they just may not be suitable for your child. But be wise about how you handle it with your teenager or child. Don't make the friend look bad, but just let your child know that you don't agree that this person would be the best choice for them.

As you follow the Spirit, He will guide and protect you and your children in the friendships they develop.

You may also get a "check" in your spirit about allowing your child to attend or participate in certain events. Your children need to be able to participate in or attend certain events, but if you get a "check" in your spirit about an event, follow that; the Spirit knows more than you do, and He is endeavoring to help you.

DECISION MAKING

It's important that your teenagers understand how important it is for you to be able to trust them. You can't trust your kids by faith. You can trust your kids only as they earn that trust; they earn trust through obeying you and through making right decisions.

The decisions your teenagers and kids make not only affect them, but many times they affect the whole family; they must be taught to understand how far-reaching the effects of their decisions can be. As your kids grow, there are more decisions they will have to make, but the parent's guidance over those decisions will have to stay nearby. Parents must guide them into what good decisions look like.

Some teenagers will press upon parents to let them make their own decisions, but they're safe in making some decisions only after they have a history of making good, right decisions. If they're repeatedly making bad, wrong decisions, that's clear proof that they're not ready to make their own decisions, no matter how old they may be. Yes, as kids grow, they must learn to make decisions, but it's best to let them practice making right decisions on the situations that aren't so important. As they succeed in those decisions, then they can be trusted with more important ones.

As a parent, there are times you will have to make decisions for your teenagers that they wouldn't make for themselves. For example, there may be times when you make the decision for them about what job they can take. Will it put them in the right kind of fellowship? Will it pull them out of church? Will it benefit them immediately? Will it benefit them in the long run? The parents will have to be a guide in these types of decisions.

FRIENDS OF THE SAME AGE

As kids enter their teen years, they are flattered by the opportunity to hang around with kids that are older. They want to impress and belong, so they are sometimes easily influenced by older kids. That's why it's important, especially during the teenage years, that teens primarily fellowship with those of their own age or within a year or so of their age. The maturity difference between a 13-year old and a 16-year old is great during those years, and it can bring difficulty for a 13-year old to fellowship in a circle of only older kids, since older kids have liberties that younger ones shouldn't have. As kids exit their teenage years, this doesn't always hold as true, but when they're younger, it's something to pay close attention to.

HONOR & RESPECT

During these teenage years, you will begin to see an expression of independence that is part of this season of their life, but the principles, guidelines and boundaries that you put in place in their younger years will have to be fortified and guarded closely, for they are all precautions for their safety and crucial for their training.

There may be a flaring up of bad attitudes that you haven't encountered before this time, but it will be the parent's responsibility to hold the young person's honor and respect in place. Their respect and honor toward you must be held in place so they will continue to follow as you lead them. People only follow when there's proper respect and honor for the one in the lead.

As I was growing up, any rolling of the eyes, stomping of the foot, slamming of the door, or wrong attitude in the voice were all things that brought you eye-to-eye with the wrath of mother. The better you held those things in check, the better life was for you. The more liberties you took toward these wrong expressions, the more liberties you lost. If you were brave enough to start it, she was brave enough to finish it! We seemed to know that she would outlast us, so it was better just not start what ought not be started. All of this was part of holding us in check so we would better follow her lead.

"WHERE ARE YOU?"

When we were growing up, we were expected to keep our parents informed at all times as to our whereabouts, and if mother felt so inspired, she didn't hesitate to follow up on us to make sure we were where we said.

If we were in a place we knew we weren't supposed to be and she found out about it, she was known to remove you from that place herself. She didn't shy away from keeping us safe.

Throughout the lives of our sons, I've made it my business to know where they were and who they were with at all times. In protecting them, I was protecting our whole family.

OBEDIENCE & PRIVILEGES

Isaiah 1:19 reads, *"If ye be WILLING AND OBEDIENT, ye shall eat the good of the land."* Willingness deals with the attitude of the heart, and obedience deals with the act of obeying. Both must be in place for you to experience the good things in life. You can obey, but it's important that obedience be accompanied with the right attitude – you have to be willing.

Ephesians 6:1-3 reads, *"Children, obey your parents in the Lord: for this is right. Honour thy father and mother; which is the first commandment with promise; THAT IT MAY BE WELL WITH THEE, AND THOU MAYEST LIVE LONG ON THE EARTH."*

When our sons obeyed and honored us, things went well with them, but when they didn't, things didn't go as well with them – they lost out on privileges they could have been enjoying.

With obedience comes blessings and privileges, but with disobedience comes loss – loss of blessings and loss of privileges. When our sons kept their obedience in place, they kept their privileges in place. If they shunned obedience, they forfeited privileges, and the choice was theirs, not ours.

When they disobeyed and lost privileges, I made them acknowledge who was to blame for their loss of privileges – the blame was theirs because the choice to disobey was theirs. I made them learn to take the responsibility when the blame was theirs, because that's the only way to fully correct the situation. True repentance acknowledges its own fault – it's not looking to blame someone else for its own failures and mistakes. This is all part of spiritual training.

Chapter Fourteen

Dating & Marriage

Some teenagers and young adults make the decision that they don't want to date, for they believe that God will bring the right person into their life when they are ready to marry. Hooray for you! God can certainly bring you the person that will be right for your life, but at some point you will have to get to know that person, even if it's not in the conventional setting of dating.

Then there are those kids who do date, so the dating life should have clearly defined guidelines and boundaries. One of the guidelines that we set for our two sons is that they are not allowed to date until they're 18 years old. But we didn't start telling them that when they were 15 years old; we told them that all the years they were growing up, so then it wasn't an ordeal as they got older – they knew the rules all along.

When they reach dating age, they aren't allowed to date anyone we don't agree to. If we don't allow them to date someone, it's not because we don't like a particular person, but because we don't think it would be of benefit to everyone.

The primary thing we consider before letting our sons date, is, "Will this person pull them away from their call?"

Another thing we consider is if the person they want to date has a good habit of church attendance? Are they active in their local church? If your kids date or marry someone who isn't interested in the local church, or doesn't have good church attendance habits, they can pull your son or daughter out of the church. These are the things that are important to us, so we have made these things a priority when it comes to our sons.

What kind of home does that girl or boy live in? Is it a home full of chaos and crisis, strife and conflict? Is it a troubled home? Do you want that kind of home to be repeated in the life of your own child?

These are all things you must consider before you give your consent to someone they want to date. If you permit them to date someone, but later realize they don't meet your standard, then you could have a difficult situation on your hands, especially if you try to stop the relationship.

The thing of primary importance is to look to the guidance of the Holy Spirit. The Spirit of God knows more than you, and He will be faithful to lead you in these situations.

HONORING THE PARENT'S OPINION

We have taught our sons that they will not date someone we don't agree to, because who they date affects us. We, as parents, never brought someone around our lives or the lives of our children who would have a negative effect on them, and we won't agree to allow our children to bring someone into their own lives who will have a negative effect on us. We have taught them to honor us by considering how their relationships affect us, their parents.

Kids must be taught that they can't be mindless and selfish about whom they invite into their lives, because whole families are affected by those connected to their lives. Therefore, train them in the way they should go when it comes to dating and marrying.

Yes, who they marry is ultimately their decision, but we refuse to let our sons approach that decision untrained. We train them in what a good decision for a mate looks like. We have taught our children that it is to matter to them that we agree with who they date or marry. We have taught them to honor their parents enough to consider our word in the matter. We've taught our children that it needs to matter to them that we're pleased with the choices they make. We don't teach them that so we can control them, but because we have their best interest at heart.

Because my husband and I are both in the ministry, the choices our sons make of whom to marry will not only affect the family, but it will affect the ministry. All this must be considered when it comes time for them to choose a spouse.

A PROPER PERSPECTIVE

Now, it's to be understood that some parents don't carry a proper perspective when it comes to their own children. In the eyes of some parents, no person is good enough for their son or daughter, so any perspective date or any serious relationship is met with automatic disapproval. That is not a healthy or realistic approach for any parent to take. God will prepare the right person for your son or daughter, but you must deal fairly and balanced in this matter if you want your child to respect your counsel and opinion.

THE RIGHT IDEA ABOUT LOVE

Young people can sometimes have the wrong idea about love. They think, "If I'm in love with someone, that means that it's the will of God for me to marry them."

NO, IT DOESN'T! If you are around the wrong people, you can fall in love with the wrong people – and God didn't have anything to do with it.

Parents, your children will fall in love with who they're around. Make sure that you pay attention to who they're around, and to who they're dating.

"GO SOUTH!"

When our oldest son was 20 years old, he decided that dating around was something he didn't want to do anymore. He came to me and said, "Mom, I'm not going to date anyone that you don't think I could marry." My husband and I had both sensed that Stephen would soon marry, so we appreciated that he had come to that decision on his own.

Not long after that, he was talking to me about someone he was interested in, so he asked, "Mom, what do you think? Do you think this girl is someone I should ask out on a date? I don't want to date anyone I couldn't marry."

I told him, "I don't know the girl enough to even give you an answer."

But day after day, he came to me asking the same question, but still I didn't have an answer for him. After he had come to me a number of times, I decided I needed to pray about this. "God, we've taught our children to have confidence in and honor for our counsel in their life. Stephen is looking for our input in this situation. So, I'm asking You for Your guidance in this situation." I prayed that simple prayer, and then I began to pray in the Spirit, in other tongues.

As I prayed in the Spirit, I quieted my mind and focused on my spirit. By doing that, my spirit was active and my mind was inactive. So, for the next twenty minutes I prayed in the Spirit. I didn't try to mentally search out my answer, but I looked to my spirit within to enlighten me. As I kept my mind quiet, the answer the Spirit of God gave to my own spirit floated up and enlightened my mind.

If my mind had been active and busy, then my mind could have missed what my spirit knew. Did you know that your own spirit knows things that your mind doesn't yet know? God communicates His will to your spirit, and then your own spirit will enlighten your mind if you'll get your mind quiet enough to hear your own spirit.

That's what I was doing that day; I was allowing my spirit to enlighten my mind.

After twenty minutes of praying in the Spirit, up floated the answer from my spirit. "The girl Stephen's asking about isn't the one. Go south!"

While growing up, my family had taken a few trips to the Deep South, so I knew what God meant. I knew that God meant to go to the southern states.

I looked at our calendar to see when we were scheduled to preach again in the south. In the upcoming months, we were scheduled to go to Alabama and to Florida, so I told my husband, "When we go to Alabama and Florida, I would like Stephen to go with us." I didn't tell Stephen what the Lord had said to me; I just told him he would be making those two trips with us.

When it came time to travel to Alabama, something came up and Stephen was unable to go. About a month after that was the Florida trip, so he went there with us.

The three of us flew into Florida and the pastors picked us up at the airport. When we got in the pastor's car, the pastor's wife turned to Stephen and asked, "Stephen, are you dating anyone?"

"No ma'am," Stephen answered.

"Well, we've got a jewel in our church, but you can't have her," she laughed.

Well, to make a long story short – he got the jewel – they're married today!

They married with our blessing, the blessing of her parents, and the blessing of her pastors.

Praying in the Spirit played a vital role in Stephen marrying the right person. What if I hadn't taken the time to pray in the Spirit? I wouldn't have received that direction and help of the Spirit.

Many times, we forfeit the help the Spirit can give us if we don't take the time to speak in other tongues, which is a divine means of communicating with God (I Corinthians 14:2). What a wonderful benefit of being a child of God and being filled with the Holy Ghost. Let's not neglect or overlook the help that the Spirit of God brings to us as parents.

Since Stephen was born, I had sensed in my spirit that he would marry someone that he met while traveling on the road with us. But by praying in the Spirit, in other tongues, greater clarity came, and God's will was made known for his life.

The decision of who to marry was Stephen's; he had to follow God's leading for himself. But as his parents, we were able to assist by praying in the Holy Ghost.

As the parent, God will not keep His will for your children hidden from you. As you stay sensitive to the Spirit of God, you can know God's plan, and you can teach your children to know God's plan for their lives.

LED BY THE SPIRIT

There have been instances when someone would give a prophecy, telling another person who they should marry. But we're not led by prophecy; we're led by the witness of the Holy Spirit in our own spirits. For Romans 8:14 & 16 says, *"For as many as are led by the Spirit of God, they are the sons of God. The Spirit itself BEARETH WITNESS WITH OUR SPIRIT... ."*

Prophecy is to only confirm what you already have in your own spirit, but it is not how God leads His children; God leads us through our own spirit. If a prophecy someone gives you doesn't confirm what you already have in your own spirit, forget it.

Even though God had spoken to me about who Stephen was to marry, I didn't tell him that. He had to be led by his own spirit as to who to marry; the decision was his, not ours.

YOU HAVE TO DO THE RIGHT THING IN THE RIGHT PLACE

Not only must we teach our children the importance of marrying right, but we must teach them the importance of doing the right thing once they do marry the right person. We can look at Adam and see the importance of this.

God created the Garden of Eden and put Adam there; Adam was in the right place because God put him there. Although Adam was in the right place, he did the wrong thing in the right place, and God had to remove him from the right place. God didn't miss it by putting Adam there; Adam missed it by doing the wrong thing in the right place.

You may be in the right place, but you have to do the right thing to stay in the right place. Getting into the right place isn't automatic, and staying in the right place isn't automatic – you have to do right. The right place must be protected by right saying and right doing.

To stay right and do right, you must maintain your own fellowship with God through feeding on the Word and prayer. Your spiritual life must be priority so you can stay on course with God's plan. Things start going wrong when the spiritual life is neglected, but things are held in place when fellowship with God is held as a priority.

DON'T WORRY

Even if it looks like your older children are making wrong decisions and going wrong directions regarding marriage or any other situation, it won't help by worrying about them. Resist the temptation to worry. Every time you're tempted to worry, say, "I refuse to worry. I cast the care of them over on the Lord, and I surround them with my faith and love. Everything will turn out alright."

Philippians 4:6 and I Peter 5:7 instructs us to not fret, worry or have any anxiety about anything, and that we're to cast all our cares on the Lord, for He cares for us. If we're worrying about it, then it's in our hands and He can't help us like He wants to. We have to get it into His hands so that He can handle the problem. Put it in His hands by refusing to worry. Tell Him that you trust Him to work in that situation, and then refuse to touch it in your thought life.

Worrying about that child won't help anything, but surrounding them with faith and love keeps the door open for God to move in their behalf. Trust God to move in their behalf.

DON'T OVERRIDE YOUR SPIRIT

God will prepare the right mate for your children, but they must follow God's leading in the matter; He will guide them. Teach your sons and daughters the importance of following their spirits when it comes to knowing God's will in marriage. As they spend time feeding on God's Word and praying in the Spirit, they can gain clarity in their spirits of the right choices to make.

When needing direction from God, many seek to hear a voice, but God seldom leads that way; they should just spend time waiting before God to gain clarity in their own spirit before they make a move.

Many have overridden what they sensed in their own spirit regarding choosing a mate, and have missed the leading of God. Even then, God will bless them as far as He can, but it's just best to follow His leading to begin with and get God's best.

Teach your children to follow their conscience, for their conscience is the voice of their own spirit speaking to them. As they follow their conscience, they will be following their spirit.

Teach your children to follow the peace within. If they don't have peace in their spirit, then they shouldn't go that direction. If there's an uneasiness in their spirit, then they shouldn't go that direction. Follow the direction of peace. Colossians 3:15 reads, *"And let the peace...from Christ rule (act as umpire continually) in your hearts [deciding and settling with finality all questions that arise in your minds..."* (Amplified Bible).

In a game of sports, the umpire's call is final. His call settles it. This scripture says that peace is to be the umpire in your spirit; it's to make the call. Follow peace and you'll make the right decision. You don't have to hear a voice from God to know His guidance; just follow the peace in your spirit – that is the leading of God.

Chapter Fifteen

Divorce & Remarriage

Parents who go through a divorce find themselves in a very unique place when raising their children. A Christian parent who has gone through a divorce is not alone; they have the help of the Holy Spirit. Learn to rely heavily upon the Holy Spirit for guidance and direction when parenting children, especially if the children have to go back and forth between parents, living in two different households.

As for any divorced Christian parent, when your children are with you, keep them in a good local church that teaches and preaches the Word. This is of utmost importance, for it keeps them in an atmosphere where the Spirit of God can minister to them. The influence of the Word and the Spirit will comfort and anchor them when they are faced with difficult situations that could unsettle them.

As you walk in the light of the Word and trust God, He will restore to you and your children that which has been lost. He can give you a home of peace and love; that's what He wants for you.

PROTECTING CHILDREN

Children of divorced parents must be protected as much as possible from the division, the conflicts, and the strife that can arise. One way to do this is to never speak negatively about your former spouse to the children. To speak ill of a former spouse around a child can force a child to have to choose between their parents, which no child should have to do. Never sow dishonor in your child toward one parent, for dishonoring a parent will affect a child negatively.

Keep the children as separated as possible from any wrong doing that may have happened during the marriage and divorce.

Always look to the Holy Spirit to lead you regarding your children when you're faced with a difficult situation as the result of a divorce; He will help you and them.

GET RID OF HURTS

When a divorce happens, the hurt and difficulties can linger if not handled right, but the Holy Spirit is the great Helper even in those times. If going through or having been through a divorce, you must forgive and not hold any ill-will against a former spouse, for you don't want to leave an open door to the enemy. To forgive is to keep the door closed to the enemy – to sickness, lack, and a host of other problems. The children must also be taught this so they don't harbor any unforgiveness or ill-will toward anyone.

Another great help during those difficult times is to spend much time praying in the Holy Ghost, in other tongues. Praying in other tongues is the way to get all the hurt out so the rest of your life isn't marked by that hurtful event. As you choose to forgive others and pray in the Spirit, He will remove that hurt and the ill effects of a relationship gone wrong. Not only will He do that for you, but He will do that for your children. Teach them to spend time praying in other tongues; even pray in tongues with them, and He will remove all the hurt.

REMARRIAGE

When remarrying, it is important that your children be of utmost consideration. Whoever you marry must love your children, and must treat them as they would their own. If they take issue with any of your children, then they will not be a suitable mate. God wants a home of love, peace and safety for your whole family, and He will give you someone that treasures you and your children. Don't settle for anything less.

If you will follow the Spirit of God when remarrying, He will lead you to marry someone who will bless your whole family – you and your children.

HOW TO RECEIVE THE INFILLING OF THE HOLY GHOST

As I stated, praying in the Holy Ghost is the way to get rid of hurts that come as the result of a broken marriage and home.

To receive the infilling of the Holy Spirit is to move into a deeper dimension of God.

Jesus is the gift that God gave the whole world. *"For God so loved the world, that he gave his only begotten Son, that WHOSO-EVER believeth in him should not perish, but have everlasting life."* Whosoever will can receive this gift, and Acts 2:21 tells us how to receive Jesus. *"...whosoever shall call on the name of the Lord shall be saved."* To call on the name of the Lord to be saved is simply to say, "Jesus, I believe you are the Son of God. You are God's gift to me, so I call you my Lord. I receive you as my Savior, therefore, I am a child of God now."

Jesus is the gift that God gave the whole world, but God has an additional gift for His own children; this gift isn't for the whole world – it's only for His children – the gift of the Holy Ghost.

Act 2 tells about when the Holy Spirit was given. When God's people received the Holy Spirit, they began to speak in other tongues.

Because the Holy Spirit is God's gift to His children, to receive the Holy Spirit is as simple as receiving any other gift that someone may give you. You can simply say, "Father, I see that the person of the Holy Spirit is a gift that you have for your children, so I receive the gift now. Thank you for filling me with the Holy Spirit. Now, since I'm filled, I expect to speak with other tongues as the Spirit gives me utterance, just as they did in the Bible."

From your spirit (not from your mind), words will float up. Speak those words out. God won't move your mouth for you, but the Spirit will give you the words to utter. Speak them out.

This gift is yours to use for the rest of your life. Every day, take time to speak in other tongues, for the benefits are great. (For more instruction on this subject, I recommend *Why Tongues* by Kenneth E. Hagin.)

THE GREAT HELPER

As you take time to speak in other tongues daily, you will be edified and built up, and the Holy Spirit will remove hurts from you.

Receiving the infilling of the Holy Spirit with the evidence of speaking in other tongues will move you into a deeper dimension of God. As you take time to speak in tongues in your everyday life, you will tap into some of the greatest help you can receive in parenting. The Holy Spirit is your great Helper, and He will help you be successful with this great privilege of parenting.

Chapter Sixteen

A Home of Peace

One of the greatest treasures in life is to have a home of peace – a home that is a safe haven, a place of refuge and a place of refreshing in a hectic, busy world. The home of peace is a place where all its occupants look forward to coming to. It's the job of the parents to set the atmosphere of the home, making it a place where the children love to be, and a place friends admire.

Because there were four kids in the home where I grew up, there was always a lot of activity, but I always remember it as being a happy place. Being raised in a smaller town, there weren't as many activities available to us, so we mostly stayed at home. It was a place where our friends were welcome, and where we were happy to be.

We certainly did our fair share of fighting with each other at times, but we knew there was a limit. If we crossed that line, then mother would get involved, and we would all be in trouble.

When mother dealt with us, she didn't raise her voice to yell and scream, although she certainly spoke firmly at times. She knew that she was in charge, and therefore, she didn't have to scream. What she said stood!

I remember going to the homes of some friends and hearing the parents yell and scream at their kids. I was always taken aback by it, because that's not the way our parents dealt with us. When a parent is always yelling and screaming, they have forgotten they are in charge. To parent that way is to set a combative atmosphere in the home. To parent that way is to teach your children to become combative. It breaks down and destroys all respect for one another in the home. It destroys the peace in the home, and as kids become old enough, they will do anything to get out of a home like that.

When we got out of line and my mother dealt with us, at times she would certainly be stern. She would set the situation right, but it wasn't through yelling and screaming at us. She would use her authority as the parent and put everything back in order. Sometimes, we got spanked, and sometimes we lost privileges, but she handled us in a way that put things back in order.

It's up to the parent to create and maintain the kind of atmosphere in the home that makes it a place of peace and happiness.

A MARRIAGE OF PEACE

To have peace in the home, there must be peace in the marriage, and that only comes by the parents being a doer of the Word. Parents must realize that they are on the same team – not opposing teams with each one trying to win their own way.

Children who are raised in a peaceful home are given a head start in life, but children who are raised in a home of turmoil where the parents are combative toward each other, are weakened. A combative marriage and home are devastating to children. It twists and breaks the hearts of children to hear the two people they love and depend upon the most to be arguing and speaking harshly to each other. Make a commitment that harshly spoken or combative words are not an option for your marriage and home. Refuse to give it a place in your life or your home. There may be times that parents need to discuss and resolve a matter, but never do it in front of children or where children can overhear. To do so is to plant difficulties in your children that can trip them up for the rest of their lives.

It's not those who hear the Word of God that are blessed in life, but those who are doers of the Word. The doing of the Word must be first and foremost in the home – the Word must find its highest expression at home among your family.

Walk in the love of God, and honor one another in your home; make your home a place of peace and a place of heaven on earth – your child's future depends on it.

Sinner's Prayer

Heavenly Father, I come to You in the Name of Jesus. Your Word says, *"...him that cometh to me I will in no wise cast out"* (John 6:37). So I know You won't cast me out; but You will take me in, and I thank You for it.

You said in Your Word, *"...If thou shalt confess with thy mouth the Lord Jesus, and shall believe in thine heart that God has raised him from the dead, thou shalt be saved...For whosoever shall call upon the name of the Lord shall be saved"* (Romans 10:9, 13).

I believe in my heart that Jesus Christ is the Son of God. I believe Jesus died for my sins and was raised from the dead so I could be in right standing with God. I am calling upon His Name, the name of Jesus, so I know that You save me now.

Your Word says, *"...with the heart man believeth unto right-eousness; and with the mouth confession is made unto salvation"* (Romans 10:10). I do believe with my heart, and I confess Jesus now as my Lord. Therefore, I am saved! Thank You, Father.

How to be Filled with the Holy Spirit

Acts 2:38 reads:
...Repent, and be baptized every one of you in the name of Jesus Christ for the remission of sins, and ye shall receive the GIFT of the Holy Ghost.

The Holy Ghost is a gift that belongs to each one of God's people. Jesus is the gift God gave the whole world, but the Holy Spirit is a gift that belongs only to God's people.

Jesus told His disciples:
But ye shall receive POWER, after that the Holy Ghost is come upon you: and ye shall be witnesses unto me.
(Acts 1:8)

When you're baptized with the Holy Spirit, you receive a supernatural power that enables you to live victoriously.

INDWELLING VS. INFILLING

When a person is born again, they receive the *indwelling* of the Holy Spirit. Romans 8:16 tells us, *"The Spirit itself beareth witness with our spirit, that we are the children of God."* When you're born again, you know it because the Spirit bears witness with your own spirit that you are a child of God, He confirms it to you. He's able to bear witness with your spirit because He's in you; you are *indwelt* by the Spirit of God.

But the Word of God speaks of another experience subsequent to the new birth that belongs to every believer, and that is to be baptized with the Holy Spirit, or to receive the *infilling* of the Holy Spirit. God wants you to be full and overflowing with the Spirit.

Being filled with the Spirit is likened to being full of water. Just because you had one drink of water doesn't mean you're full of

95

water. At the new birth you received the *indwelling* of the Spirit – a drink of water. But now God wants you to be filled to overflowing – be filled with His Spirit, baptized with the Holy Ghost.

Acts 2:1-4 reads:
And when the day of Pentecost was fully come, they were all with one accord in one place. And suddenly there came a sound from heaven as of a rushing mighty wind, and it filled all the house where they were sitting. And there appeared unto them cloven tongues like as of fire, and it sat upon each of them. And they were all FILLED with the Holy Ghost, and BEGAN TO SPEAK WITH OTHER TONGUES, as the Spirit gave them utterance.

When these disciples were filled with the Holy Ghost, they began to speak with other tongues as the Spirit gave them utterance. Today, when a believer receives the infilling of the Holy Spirit, they also will speak with other tongues. These are not words that come from the mind of man, but they are words that will float up from their spirit, and the person then speaks those out.

Matthew 7:7-11 reads:
Ask, and it shall be given you...For every one that asketh receiveth...what man is there of you, whom if his son ask bread, will he give him a stone? Or if he ask a fish, will he give him a serpent? If ye then, being evil, know how to give good gifts unto your children, how much more shall your Father which is in heaven give good things to them that ask him?

In this passage, Jesus is telling us that when you ask God for something, you shall receive! Believe that He will give you that which you ask for. When you ask God for something good, He won't give you something that will harm you; He will give you the good thing you ask for. The Holy Spirit is a good gift, and when you ask

God to fill you with the Holy Spirit, you won't receive a wrong spirit; you will receive this good gift, the gift of the Holy Spirit.

Since the Holy Spirit is a gift, once you receive it, it's yours to use any time you choose. You can yield to this gift, the Holy Spirit within you, and speak in tongues as often as you choose; you don't have to wait for God to move on you. Those who neglect speaking in other tongues will diminish in fullness, but by continuing to speak in other tongues on a daily basis, you will be able to maintain a Spirit-filled life; you will stay full of the Spirit.

The more you take time to speak in other tongues, the deeper you'll move into the things of God.

(For more teaching on being filled with the Holy Spirit, I recommend *Why Tongues* by Kenneth E. Hagin.)

PRAYER TO BE FILLED WITH THE HOLY SPIRIT

Father, I see that the Holy Spirit is a gift that belongs to Your children. So, I come to You now to receive the Holy Spirit. I received my salvation by faith, so now I receive the gift of the Holy Spirit by faith. I believe I receive the Holy Spirit now!

Since I'm filled with the Holy Spirit now, I expect to speak in other tongues as the Spirit gives me utterance, just like those in Acts 2 on the Day of Pentecost. Thank You for filling me with the Holy Ghost.

Now, from your spirit, words that the Spirit of God is giving will float up. You are the one who must open your mouth and speak those words out. They are not words that will pass through your mind, but they float up from your spirit. Speak those out freely.

Fit for the Master's Use